# Executives Praise *Drive Profits Today*:

**Bret Schnitker, CEO, Stars Design Group**
**Global Apparel – *starsdesigngroup.com***
*"Craig and Steven remind us concisely how to apply fundamentals to grow profitably in a fast-paced and hurried, modern landscape. The common sense dialogue transcends borders and industries."*

**Bill Hinderer, President, Tacony Corporation**
**Home and Commercial Products – *tacony.com***
*"With the economy improving, the emphasis is now on driving profits by growing top line sales. This book shares simple, practical action items that can help you make that happen."*

**Kevin Haar, CEO, Appistry**
**Genomics Medicine Data – *appistry.com***
*"It's rewarding to read a book that is simply helpful. Drive Profits Today doesn't try to tell you how to be a corporate leader, but instead, reminds you of lessons learned while bringing new tools to your toolbox. The customer-centric orientation through the eyes of a CEO bring a perspective that is direct and refreshing."*

**Jarrett Koltoff, CEO, SpearTip**
**Global Cyber Counterintelligence – *speartip.com***
*"Drive Profits Today hits on the key fundamentals critical for successful growth in today's challenging marketplace. These tips apply to everyone within the organization regardless of industry and size."*

**Rusty Keeley, CEO, The Keeley Companies**
**National Construction Services – *lkeeley.com***
*"The Palubiaks put everything into perspective for growing an organization while driving profits. They provide excellent tips for assessing company alignment and gaining focused commitment to the Mission as well as targeted customers. Their common sense tips are easily implemented and the simple process of accountable action plans ensure success!"*

**Chris Adderton, Vice President**
**Council of Supply Chain Management Professionals (CSCMP)**
**Global Trade Association – *cscmp.org***
*"Drive Profits Today clearly describes how to move from strategy to tactics and effectively convert effort and ideas into profitable results. Using the process outlined, you will gain alignment and focus in this dynamic market environment."*

**David Payne, President, PayneCrest Electric**
**National Engineering Services – *paynecrest.com***
*"Drive Profits Today provides practical tips to engage employees in fulfilling the corporate mission and empower them to build and sustain personal relationships with customers and prospects that are the life blood of any business."*

**John O'Rourke, Chairman, O&R Medical Sales and Service**
**Medical Supplies – *ormedical.com***
*"This book is a concise overview of the issues implicit in driving profits today. Although it is a quick read it offers a substantive and thought provoking analysis of the business policies and actions that separate successful businesses from those that fail."*

**Peter Desloge, CEO & Chairman, Watlow**
**Global Manufacturer – *watlow.com***
*"Drive Profits Today is written from the perspective of the CEO. It is a straight forward, no nonsense book filled with practical ideas that can quickly be implemented and most importantly starts with the customer. This is a great read for a team wanting to get aligned to grow their business."*

**Michael Gallagher, Area Managing Director, Accenture**
**Global Consulting Firm – *accenture.com***
*"Not often does a book of common sense come along, that is written in easily digestible and more importantly, actionable style as Drive Profits Today."*

**Clayton Brown, CEO, The International Companies**
**Food Ingredients – *ifpc.com***
*"The Palubiaks give you common sense tips to help your company and employees become aligned in order to ultimately satisfy the needs of your customers and drive your company's profitable growth."*

**Lauren Herring, CEO, IMPACT Group**
**Global Career Development – *impactgrouphr.com***
*"The Palubiaks quickly identify critical issues for growing profitable companies whether they are regional, national or global. Successful teams are in alignment and focused on a common mission. They target the right customers and deliver the right value proposition."*

## Purpose

This book shares tips that will help your entire organization (the marketing and sales teams in particular) achieve your corporate goals. Each tip consists of thought-provoking questions, real-world examples, and action items that your team can implement immediately, whether you are dealing with B2B or B2C, domestic or global, small or large clients.

**Copyright © 2018, 2014**

**Craig Palubiak**
**Steven Palubiak**

Printed in the United States of America
10 9 8 7 6 5 4 3 2 1

ISBN:  1-893308-15-4
ISBN:  978-1-893308-15-2

Optim Consulting Group
optimgroupusa.com
St. Louis, Missouri

*Dedicated to your profitable growth...*

# Table of Contents

# Foreword

Ownership and executive management teams throughout the globe routinely discuss how best to maximize their company's valuation. Profitable growth is frequently the first response whether it is to be accomplished organically or through mergers and acquisitions. The latter is dependent upon strong financial resources and the ability to outbid other suitors. The former is estimated to represent nearly 70% of all such growth. *Drive Profits Today – Timeless Sales and Marketing Tips* is designed to benefit the leadership and stakeholders in both scenarios. The following represent tips highlighted in this book:

» Confirming team alignment with your customer

» Understanding the rapidly evolving new customer

» Targeting prospects and clients by title hot buttons

» Outwitting the competition through market intelligence

» CUSTOMERization results in optimal customer selection

The successful companies will be those that quickly get their teams in alignment and proactively pursue profitable growth whether it is with B2B or B2C, domestic or global, small or large clients.

*Craig Steven*

# Introduction

Benjamin Franklin said it so well 200 years ago, "Drive thy business, or it will drive thee!"

Whether you are new to business, or a veteran, you have undoubtedly realized how challenging the customer is in this dynamically changing world. Today's customers are better informed, more sophisticated and demanding, and less loyal than ever. Competing for business requires more than selling a product or service. It mandates a constant reevaluation of what works and what does not. And then adapting instantly. Quite simply, your team must drive thy business, if you are to Drive Profits Today!

This book begins with the critical issue of all team members being on the same page and working towards a common goal. Your marketing and sales teams are paramount to this success.

Marketing has become much more complex with the advancement of technology. It employs social media tools such as Twitter, YouTube and Facebook for evaluating items including market needs, distribution channels, promotional campaigns, competition and sales data in an effort to find and satisfy targeted customers.

Yet, these tools may change or become antiquated almost overnight.

Your sales team's role is to leverage your marketing and bring the human relationship aspect to your clients and prospective clients. If your sales team is not effective in communicating and earning trust, you are doomed to fail.

Whatever your function might be within the company, read these tips with an open mind. A few might be out of your comfort zone. Try them anyway. On the other hand, some of the tips will appear to be "common sense." Ask yourself: *"Are we currently executing these tips? If not, should we and how soon can we get started?"*

This book will cover:

## 1. Company Assessment
*Are We In Alignment*

The Critical Issues Assessment is an excellent tool for gathering information to verify whether your team is in alignment. It combines a SWOT analysis with anonymous team feedback that will produce an accurate picture about where to focus your company's improvement energies as you strive to satisfy customer needs.

## 2. Mission Statements
*The Ultimate Sales Tool*

While mission statements are often overlooked, they play one of the most imperative roles to your success. Not only do they enhance company culture they are also the ultimate sales tool, if used correctly.

## 3. The Height of Ingratitude
*The New Customer*

Today's customer continues to become better informed, more demanding, shrewder and busier than ever before. This pace of change will only accelerate as technology brings the world closer together. The successful companies will support their entire team in using these tools to maximize customer focus. They will maintain an ongoing partnership with the tough new customer.

## 4. Targeting Prospects & Clients By Title
*What Are The Hot Buttons*

It is no surprise that different people you want to sell to (or sell more to) have different hot button issues and operating styles. What issues are likely to be important to each key constituency, and how do you build relationships at multiple levels with the appropriate members of your team?

## 5. Learning Prospect & Client Needs
*Filling The Voids*

The Value-Performance Grid allows customers to provide a "weighting" factor for those issues that they value most. This maximizes the effectiveness of your assessments and helps both your marketing and sales teams in delivering exceptional results that will allow you to beat the competition!

## 6. Activating Intrapreneurship
*Driving Creative Approaches*

Empower your employees with the freedom to think outside the box. You hired them for a reason, so empower them and leverage their resources! This type of approach is known as intrapreneurship, which is creating a culture of openness and creativity among your team members.

## 7. Knowledge Source
*Beyond Features & Benefits*

The issue many sales people have is that they hide behind the illusory safety of features and benefits without first asking questions and having a dialogue with the buyer. To be effective, you must stop assuming you know what your potential buyer is looking for. Ask questions to learn more and build a trusting relationship as a knowledge source.

## 8. Competitive Intelligence
*Outwitting The Competition*

You can't talk about making a profit without knowing your competition. They are out there and they want your customers, so you better not be complacent, or they will succeed! Just like you need to learn about your target market, you have to learn about your competition.

## 9. CUSTOMERizaton
*Customer Selection*

Be cautious not to take all of the competitions' customers. You do not want everyone. Remember your mission statement and use that to be selective in who you target. This tactic is called CUSTOMERization. It simply means identifying and serving what you perceive as your targeted customers and politely firing your bottom tier. As a result, you will be happier and more profitable than you could ever imagine!

# » TIP 1
## Company Assessment
*Are We In Alignment*

Driving profitable growth requires that your team is in alignment internally and externally regarding the issues that are vital to the smooth and efficient operation of your company with the ultimate goal of fulfilling customer expectations. This entails the full range of items including, but not limited to your corporate strategy and goals, process flow, information systems, personnel, products and services.

In essence, your sales and marketing efforts will result in sustained profitable growth only if they are properly integrated and supported throughout the entire organization. Customer satisfaction in the form of new and repeat purchases is the ultimate measure of such alignment.

Harold O'Shea Builders is a thriving construction services firm located in Central Illinois. Founded in 1902, the O'Shea family's fourth generation of leadership fully understands team alignment. The management and employees are routinely asked how the team can best serve the needs of its clients and they agree on key areas of improvement. This process is completed internally as well as with third party facilitators. The result of listening to the team has been sustained growth even during times of economic turmoil.

Ask a Harold O'Shea Builder's team member to recite the company mission statement and most likely the response will be verbatim:

*"Our mission is to advance our client's goals and build lasting relationships through quality construction projects."*

The Harold O'Shea team does not only know and believe in their mission, they continually live it by aligning themselves with their clients. The result is a continuous stream of new and repeat clients.

"Drive thy business, or it will drive thee."

Benjamin Franklin

# Pain and/or Desire = Need

Business fundamentally exists to satisfy customers' needs and those needs invariably change over time. You must continuously probe to determine where your customers and prospects have pain and/or desire. These are the two drivers that create the need. Whenever there is pain there is a need for relief. And whenever there is desire, there is a need to fulfill that desire. In either case, your quick and accurate assessment spells opportunity.

By listening to both your management and associates, you gain first-hand knowledge as to how you are performing in satisfying these marketplace needs. The perceptions of your team are critical for verifying whether your team is alignment.

# Feedback Mechanisms

The first step is gathering management feedback. Management must stay closely in tune with both the employees and marketplace. In today's dynamically changing world, it is imperative that management not isolate itself in the ivory tower (or warehouse). Management must be seen, listening and interacting everywhere!

The second step is to have open dialogue with your employees. Whether they are referred to as associates, partners or team members, these individuals represent the ultimate link between management and the marketplace. They are a critical component in providing instant feedback on whether your company is offering the desired products and services. And whether your offerings are being delivered as promised in the eyes of the client.

As opportunities and issues of concern surface, the associate should be made to feel comfortable in delivering information and opinions within the organization. The freedom and ability to openly communicate, regardless of one's title or social standing, is absolutely essential.

Ongoing feedback mechanisms can be designed in a free-flowing format, or structured on a more formal basis including written messages, verbal exchanges, email and so forth. Management can prioritize these communications in such a way that some issues can be discussed spontaneously, while others can be addressed on a more formal basis, such as scheduling meeting times.

# Critical Issues Assessment

In addition to ongoing feedback from the team, a formal audit of perceptions of critical issues under the guidance of an outside facilitator can provide valuable information. Known as the Critical Issues Assessment, the audit can either be completed by all the associates and management, or by a sampling of those in various parts of the company. This assessment has become an integral tool in many a company's quest to realize their goals.

The Critical Issues Assessment provides feedback regarding those "critical issues" that will produce an accurate picture about where to focus the company's improvement energies as it strives to satisfy its customers. Individual participants should be assured that their responses will be collected anonymously.

The assessment can be designed to meet the particular needs of any organization. The following sections have proved valuable in covering the issues effecting most companies in identifying areas where there is room for improvement in terms of company alignment.

Regardless of the method used to get everyone on the same page, the necessity of doing so is indisputable. Unless marketing and sales are in alignment with the rest of the company's team, and vice versa, the organization will be unable to deliver a consistently positive customer experience resulting in profitable growth!

# Critical Issues Assessment: Section 1

The first part of the assessment is to ask the participants to rank various issues (usually about 20) from most important to least important for the long-term success of the business. These are ranked in a format such as from number 1 (most important) to number 20 (least important). Each number should be used only once. Typical issues include:

» Company mission and goals

» Company culture and team effort

» Rewards and recognition

» Product and service quality

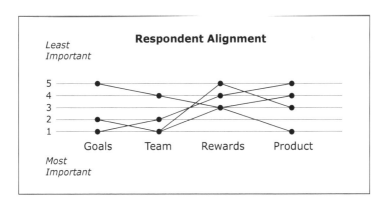

The next step is to identify which of the 3 rated issues offer the greatest current opportunity for improvement to better serve the clients.

# Critical Issues Assessment: Section 2

Section two consists of a series of open-ended questions. A common thread among these questions is the issue of how the participants perceive their personal roles relative to the company mission statement. Of equal importance is the question of what role the participants perceive their superiors play (or should play) within the organization. Questions for this section might include:

» What is the company mission statement?

» What is your role within the organization?

» Do you fulfill your role?

» What is the role of your boss?

» Does your boss fulfill the role as described?

» How might your roles better assist you both in helping the company best satisfy its customers' needs, and ultimately reach your company's goals?

# Critical Issues Assessment: Section 3

The primary purpose of this section is to identify the strengths and weaknesses of the company as perceived by the participants. There are several questions that should be answered here, including the following:

» Do the participants agree by department, division and/or universally, on the strengths and weaknesses of the company? If so, what are they? If not, what is the range of opinion and why is there disagreement?

» What can be done to improve the company's performance in satisfying its customers' needs, and ultimately reach your company's goals?

# Example

Ford Motor Company's recent turnaround was based on creating company-wide alignment in understanding and satisfying its customers' needs. As part of that alignment effort, Ford CEO Alan Mulally required weekly meeting attendance from the head of every Ford unit around the world, either in-person or via teleconference. The business unit heads had to answer the CEO's questions regarding what they were hearing from their employees and customers and how best to leverage this feedback.

The most prevailing feedback was that Ford must dramatically improve product quality if it were to survive. This amounted to a requirement that the executives align themselves on all quality related issues with their individual teams—immediately! The result of aligning this huge enterprise on the cultural value of quality has been massive increases in profitable sales.

# Summary

Driving profitable growth requires that your team is in alignment internally and externally regarding the issues that are vital to the smooth and efficient operation of your company with the ultimate goal of fulfilling customer expectations.

Management must stay closely in tune with both the employees and marketplace. In today's dynamically changing world it is imperative that management not isolate itself in the ivory tower (or warehouse). Management must be seen, listening and interacting everywhere!

The Critical Issues Assessment is an excellent method for gathering this information. It provides feedback that will produce an accurate picture about where to focus your company's improvement energies as you strive to satisfy your customers.

## Action Item

**»** Identify a cross section of your management and employee team to participate in a Critical Issues Assessment with a third party facilitator. Upon completion review the results with the team and determine what action plans should be implemented.

_____

_____

_____

_____

_____

_____

_____

_____

# » TIP 2
## Mission Statements
*The Ultimate Sales Tool*

To succeed in today's rapidly changing marketplace a company must create and live by its mission statement. The mission statement is critical for properly aligning your entire team with the ultimate goal of fulfilling customer expectations.

In the business-to-business market it is equally important that your team learns to market and sell to companies only after they have investigated the prospect's mission statement. Once you identify that a prospect's mission aligns closely with yours, you have an essential advantage in the selling process. Not only that, you've laid the groundwork for a strategic long-term partnership, not just a short-term sale.

Broadly speaking, the business world can be divided into two camps: those companies that create and live a mission, and those companies that do not. Southwest Airlines is a great example of a company that has created a mission to serve both the business and consumer markets.

Take a look at its mission statement:

*"We are dedicated to the highest quality
of Customer Service delivered with a sense
of warmth, friendliness, individual pride and
Company Spirit."*

Southwest's mission statement carries major strategic implications. First, it aligns the team internally to a common purpose which is to be the best, most customer-friendly company in the airline industry (implicit). Second, it sets a standard for its passengers (customers) so that they can compare Southwest's to its product/ service delivery. Embracing this mission statement has led to many decades of profitable growth for Southwest.

**"Think mission before commission!"**

Mark Victor Hansen

# The Ultimate Sales Tool

It is vitally important that everyone, in all departments, up and down your organization, know and understand your own corporate mission. By the same token, it is crucial that your sales and marketing people know and understand your customer's corporate mission. What is it and what does it mean? Where are the key points of contact with your own mission? And more importantly, do both organizations practice what they preach?

If you can answer those questions, you are well positioned to use your company's mission statement as a powerful marketing and sales tool. You will be able to assess whether you are spending time with the right customers, and if so, how best to reinforce your position relative to both of your missions. For instance: *"We provide a quality, valued service as do you, our customer. We are a low-cost supplier, as are you."* This is a powerful entry point to the conversation! It touches their hot buttons.

Another example is that of a consumer products sales team that gained the respect of the senior buyers within one of the largest retailers in the United States. They demonstrated how closely they were aligned with the mission of the prospect. They did this by simply displaying both their mission statements simultaneously on poster boards during a sales presentation. As a result, they were able to create a solid opening discussion that led to a long-term relationship.

## Core Questions

Do you currently have a mission statement? What is your mission? If you randomly ask ten employees at your company to recite the mission statement would they all give the same response? And would they agree that it is being properly implemented? If not, there's a problem! Even if you think that your employees know and believe in your mission it is good to review periodically with your team.

# Four Classic Mistakes

There are four very common mistakes companies make when they set out to create a mission statement. Let's look at each in turn so that you learn to avoid them.

A common mistake is when the company's leadership decides having a mission statement would be "cool." However, no effort is made to consider the employees' perspective. Management develops its new revelation in a vacuum, and announces the concept at a staff meeting. This is known as the **vacuum syndrome**. Management misses the opportunity to gain insights from the rest of the organization. For example, what if the sales team could have warned management that the entire marketplace was changing and how it impacts the mission?

A second classic mistake is known as the **publication syndrome**. This occurs when the creator of the mission statement is looking to publish a book. The mission statement loses purpose as it grows into a novel-length tome. The authors include every detail possible. In this scenario, management loses sight of the mission and becomes wrapped up in details that are irrelevant.

A third common mistake is known as the **nearsighted syndrome**. This occurs when management decides implementing a mission statement will be a great way to quickly motivate the rank-and-file about some short-term issue. This could be as simple as boosting revenues or profits by the next quarter. Management doesn't care who is involved in mission development, as long as it is rolled out promptly. The problem here is that the mission statement is focused on short-term goals, rather than long-term purpose.

The fourth classic mistake is the **impossible dream syndrome**. This does not limit employee involvement in the creation of the mission statement. It is concise, motivating, and well received by the entire team. However, this syndrome goes beyond being a "stretch" goal. It is literally impossible! The consequence of the impossible dream syndrome is that the mission will quickly be deemed impractical, and apathy will set in throughout the organization. This occurred when a small local distributor announced: *"We will become the world's largest supplier of industrial valves."* The team quickly realized the statement was impractical, and therefore worthless.

# The Right Approach

Your company mission statement is the verbalization of your ideal company. It should represent a crystallization of your present and future. It should conjure up feelings of excitement and pleasure. It should become a well focused picture in your mind and be shared equally by your team.

While creating the mission statement may take only a few days, it routinely takes as much as six to nine months to fully integrate within a company. The mission statement should define why your company exists. Engage your entire company. If necessary, update an existing mission statement. Avoid any of the four mistakes you just read. And keep the statement under 50 words.

During this process, several fundamental questions must be answered:

» What is our business?

» Who is our customer?

» What is our customer's perception of value?

» How will our business be shaped in the future?

Management guru Peter Drucker said that the mission statement should also be shaped in accordance with the following five critical factors:

» Your company's history of direction and achievements

» The current preference of your company's ownership and management

» Influences of your market environment

» Limits of your company's resources

» Your company's distinctive competencies

Once you have created a mission that inspires and engages your team, the next task is to integrate it. That means learning to live it throughout the organization, and believe it internally. This is not merely a function of top management, but a matter of constant reinforcement and buy-in from everyone. Selecting vendors and job candidates that are in alignment with the company mission are examples of integration.

Remember, the goal now is to learn to pay close attention to your prospects' and clients' mission statements and find the alignment and/or overlaps! If none exists does it make sense to even be business partners? Or what would it take to get into alignment?

# Example

The following mission statements have resulted in McDonalds and Applied Materials successfully attracting customers who are in alignment with their team purpose:

*"McDonald's mission is to be the best quick service restaurant experience. Being the best means providing outstanding quality, service, cleanliness, and value, so that we make every customer in every restaurant smile."*

*"Applied Material's mission is to be the leading supplier of semiconductor fabrication solutions worldwide through innovation and enhancement of customer productivity with systems and service solutions."*

# Summary

While creating the mission statement may take only a few days, it routinely takes as much as six to nine months to fully integrate within a company. The mission statement should define why your company exists. Engage your entire company. If necessary, update an existing mission statement. Avoid any of the four mistakes you just read. And keep the statement under 50 words.

Use your company's mission statement as a powerful marketing and sales tool. You will be able to assess whether you are spending time with the right prospects and customers, and if so, how best to reinforce your position relative to both of your missions. If none exists, does it make sense to even do business together? Or what would it take to get into alignment?

_____

_____

_____

_____

_____

_____

_____

_____

## » TIP 3
## The Height Of Ingratitude
*The New Customer*

The customer continues to become better informed, more demanding, shrewder and busier than ever before. Over the past century, this developmental process has been occurring at an increasingly faster pace in the United States. In the rest of the world it has been happening as well, but at varying speeds whether it is Europe, South America or Asia.

The accelerating demands of the changing customer profile are not going to slow down, just as you are not going to slow down in your demands of your suppliers. Therefore, your company will only succeed in realizing its goals relative to market share, revenues and profitability if it truly understands and meets the ever-changing demands of your customers.

Amazon consistently ranks among the best companies globally in understanding and satisfying customers. Since 1995, this on-line retail giant has catered to its customers by wrapping cutting edge technology around the ever-changing demands of its customers. Its user-friendly website, along with low prices, no-hassle returns, free-shipping options and human touch, has resulted in nearly 10 million items being purchased daily. This is an example of being on top of the game.

"You are already sharply aware of the phenomenon of the new consumer, because you are one. On behalf of yourself or your company, you are almost certainly a better informed, more demanding, shrewder, and busier buyer than ever before. Now multiply yourself by billions worldwide and you begin to see the scope of what is happening and how it changes the game for every business on earth."

Marshall Loeb, Retired Editor, Fortune

# Evolution of the Customer

Reviewing America's history over the past century-plus will provide some perspective as to how and why the American customer has evolved. This will enable you to become better prepared for marketing both domestically and abroad. There are six periods of time that should be considered:

# Production Era (Late 1800s)

The Production Era was represented by two distinctive customers—the urban city dweller and the rural farmer. In both cases, leisure time was limited due to the need to work long hard hours, often seven days a week, in an effort to generate enough funds to cover the family's basic expenses. Children rarely received education beyond the basic primary grades because their time was spent as breadwinners. Discretionary income was frequently nonexistent. The family was under-educated, and consequently, not sophisticated as buyers.

Due to the lack of antitrust laws, the marketplace was dominated by monopolies. Therefore, customers had limited selection in many of their purchases. The theme for business was simply to produce the basic products that consumers could afford and would buy.

# Sales Era (Early to Middle 1900s)

This period included both World War I and World War II. During this time antitrust laws, child labor laws, and collective bargaining laws came into existence. Thanks in part to technology transfers from our military efforts, the customer made great gains as a buyer.

The traditional family was at its peak. While Dad worked, Mom stayed home with the kids. The school system blossomed and everyone had the chance to become educated. Firms began to advertise through the new technologies of the day—radio and television—in an effort to make gains against a host of new competitors.

Companies had to do nothing more than offer an "adequate product." Consumers had money and appetites. They wanted products. Henry Ford's mass production capabilities evidenced technological developments that allowed firms to meet expanding consumer demands. The reward for satisfying the growing demands of the marketplace was unprecedented financial success. The theme was to out produce and out sell the competition.

# Quality Era (1970s)

During the 1970s, it became apparent that something was wrong with the quality of American products. The domestic automotive industry became a focal point of this concern. Consumers came to realize that German and Japanese made cars were of higher quality than those made by Chrysler, Ford and General Motors. In many cases the imports were also less expensive!

The "Quality Movement" began seriously in the United States in the early 1970s when the quality gurus, including Edwards Deming, gained the attention of American manufacturers such as Motorola. They came to recognize that the customer expected high product quality, and that products not meeting those higher expectations were eliminated from consideration by the customer.

Service quality, too, became a key area of concern. The entire process for delivering goods and services; the "how you get it" component, became as critical as "what you get." Firms such as Honda and Disney took the lead.

# Marketing Era (1980s)

The Marketing Era was a period when business came to realize that selling alone was not sufficient for success. Business needed a more sophisticated approach to winning over customers. Otherwise, it could not realize the critical goals of increasing market share, revenues and profitability.

It became apparent to companies that the customer and marketplace had to be researched carefully before new products and services were developed. Selling alone was no longer a guaranteed ticket to large payoffs. The customer not only had become educated as a buyer, but also had numerous companies and products from which to choose. Business had to think in terms of not just selling the product, but also in terms of learning what the marketplace really wanted before going into production.

# Customer Focus Era (1990s)

The 1990s brought the era of the "tough new consumer," and the principle of demanding more and getting it! As we have seen, Marshall Loeb, Retired Editor of Fortune magazine, captured this era perfectly when he stated, *"You are almost certainly a better informed, more demanding, shrewder, and busier buyer than ever before."*

This change placed a new burden on businesses if they expected to remain competitive in any market. The winners learned that they must work in partnership with the buyer regardless of whether that buyer was a consumer or represented an organization. Businesses could only succeed if they understood and anticipated the ever-changing needs and demands of the marketplace. They had to be immersed in a customer-focused philosophy if they expected to surpass the competition.

As we consider the task of becoming customer-focused, it is helpful to review some of the research reports produced by organizations such as the Technical Assistance Research Project (TARP). TARP found that companies that focus on delivering superior service are able to command higher prices, and ultimately, realize higher profits, greater sales volume growth and greater market share growth than their competitors.

Furthermore,

» 96% of unhappy customers never complain to the supplying company about their poor service.

» Every dissatisfied customer will share his story with at least nine other people.

» 60 – 90% of the customers who are dissatisfied with the service they receive will never return.

# Digital Era (2000s)

The much-hyped Y2K scare prior to the turn of the second millennium resulted, not in disaster, but in a global explosion of information technology. Thereafter, the norm for doing business was to be radically changed frequently, and on short notice as the usage of the internet, web, digital imaging, social networks and other creations captured the imagination, and the pocketbooks of the masses.

Customers could now be reached instantaneously and they could similarly reach out to suppliers of products and/or services.  E-marketing, e-sales, on-line sourcing through such entities as eBay and Amazon resulted in a paradigm shift in how the customer was to be marketed and sold. And the paradigm is changing almost daily in some sectors with such social media tools as Facebook and Twitter.

# Example

A man lost his job. After six months he was still jobless and had used up his entire savings. He desperately needed $1,000. His minister said to pray, but he got no results. So he decided to go direct to the Lord. He wrote a tearful letter asking for $1,000. He addressed the letter to God and mailed it stampless.

The postman, thinking it was a child's letter, opened it. After reading it, he was deeply touched and took it that night to his Rotary meeting. They immediately drained their treasury of $250, and then emptied their pockets collecting $250 more. They proudly sent the $500.

A few days later, the postman found another letter like the first. He opened it and read: *God, thanks for the money, but please next time, send it to the United Way, because the Rotary stole half of it!*

Yes, sometimes it is very difficult to satisfy the demanding customer. So where do you begin?

# Summary

The customer continues to become better informed, more demanding, shrewder and busier than ever before both domestically and abroad. This pace of change will only accelerate as technology brings the world closer together.

The successful companies are customer focused throughout the entire organization. They deliver not only a quality product and quality service, but also stay in close contact with customers at all levels through the most current technology. They maintain an ongoing partnership with the tough new customer, a partnership that must be continuously nurtured.

## Action Item

» Have your team identify three clients whose partnership can be further enhanced by technology. Discuss the solutions and the best manner for implementation.

# » TIP 4

## Targeting Prospects & Clients By Title
*What Are the Hot Buttons*

Remember that your business exists to satisfy your market's ever-changing needs. In order to accomplish this, you and your team must continuously identify where there is pain and desire. In either case, your quick and accurate assessment spells opportunity.

When listening to your prospects and clients, you gain knowledge as to what keeps them up at night. Continue to ask questions, listen and provide solutions! You are not only selling to them, you are their partner and knowledge source. Step back for a moment and consider what's most important to this person. What are the typical hot buttons for their functional business position? Where does he or she want to be in their career in one, five or ten years? What kinds of allies and partnerships is this person looking for to enhance their visibility and career trajectory?

Consider Automatic Data Processing, Inc. (ADP) which is one of the world's largest providers of business data processing solutions including payroll and benefits administration. They routinely, and strategically, target numerous individuals within the companies they call on when selling services by anticipating each person's pain or desire.

Smaller company targets include the CEO/Owner. Larger company targets routinely include the CFO/Administration, Production/Operations Manager and Director of Information Systems. The ADP team is ready to discuss the relevant business issues by functional position with each of these contacts while being conscious of their different personal issues.

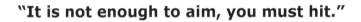

**"It is not enough to aim, you must hit."**

Italian proverb

## Pre-Visit Homework

Everyone you meet with will have a unique story, motivations and needs. It's beneficial that you know as much as possible about each person before you meet with them. Technology has made this powerful concept incredibly simple. Before you meet with a prospect or client, learn about them through search engines and social media. Look for articles, previous jobs, education, interests, etc. Leverage this knowledge by making connections with your common interests, backgrounds, professional associates and mutual acquaintances.

Even if you can't find anything, or have limited time, don't worry! There are a few key items to remember that effect everyone. Job titles often provide base-line information for addressing common hot buttons issues.

## What Are the Hot Buttons?

In this section, you'll learn about the common concerns that are likely to unite players within several of the key functional areas your marketing and sales teams will be encountering. This is not to discount any specific research your team has done, of course. Nor is it to discount the distinct special qualities of any company or buyer.

While it is true that all buyers may have a uniqueness about them, it is also true that communicating with one person on the assumption they have the same concerns as someone with very different responsibilities may needlessly lengthen (or sabotage!) your selling cycle.

Whenever possible, you should strive to talk to more than one key player within an account. In fact, several members of your team should be strategically aligned to interact with different members of your account by title and/or operating style. This increases the odds of building strong intertwined relationships while minimizing the risk if one individual within the account is torpedoing the relationship. Talk about the issue(s) of greatest interest to these individuals. Hot buttons are meant to be pushed!

Look at the list below and compare them to the people you have identified. You'll probably see some overlap because the fundamental issues tend to stay the same within a given role.

## Common Hot Button Issues by Title

| CEO | CFO | HR |
|---|---|---|
| Revenues | Revenues | Personnel |
| Cash Flow | Cash Flow | Scheduling |
| Operating Profit | Operating Profit | Monitoring |
| Market Trends | Tax Benefit | Vulnerability |

| Sales | Operations | IT |
|---|---|---|
| Revenue | Scheduling | Scheduling |
| Market Trends | Monitoring | Monitoring |
| Deliverables | Inventory | Deliverables |
| Competition | Deliverables | Vulnerability |

» **Revenues** – Where is the money coming from? What products, services and solutions will produce more liquidity for the enterprise?

» **Cash Flow** – What is the short-term financial picture? If loans/financing is an issue, is the bank happy with the cash-flow picture?

» **Operating Profit** – What's the bottom line? How is the enterprise performing against expectations and targets? Are the key stakeholders happy?

» **Tax Benefit** – How can the company create an effective, legal tax strategy that maximizes performance?

» **Market Trends** – What will the market look like six months, a year or two years from now? What technologies and social changes are likely to effect buying patterns?

» **Monitoring** – What oversight/quality control processes are in place? How can errors and inefficiencies be reduced?

» **Personnel** – What are current needs for people by position? What is their compensation package? What and how do we provide the appropriate training?

» **Competition** – What is the competition up to? How can the prospect's company establish or maintain a competitive edge?

» **Scheduling** – What is going to happen next in this person's world? What's going to happen after that? What sequence of events makes the most sense for the week/month/quarter/year?

» **Deliverables** – Who has to get what and when? What's the most cost-effective way to make sure they get it?

» **Vulnerability** – What are potential risks to our business? What is the impact of pending lawsuits and outside intrusion within our information systems?

## Example

Wagner Portrait Group is a 35 year old school photography company. Faced with a fiercely competitive market, the company's management knows how important it is to identify all the influencers within the buying process and address the relevant hot button issues. The business-to-business discussion involves the district superintendent, school principal and department heads, while the end-customer discussion includes both parents and students.

The Wagner sales team diligently does its pre-visit homework prior to making sales presentations to the school representatives. This includes learning the school mission as well as the individual's school responsibilities, educational background, experience and mutual acquaintances who might provide insights on how best to serve this person's needs.

# Summary

Different people within the companies you want to sell to (or sell more to) have different hot button issues and operating styles. Know the issues that are likely to be important to each key constituency, and build relationships at multiple levels with the appropriate members of your team!

And before you meet these individuals learn about them! Look for articles, previous jobs, education, interests, etc. Leverage this knowledge by making connections with your common interests, backgrounds, professional associates and mutual acquaintances.

Where does he or she want to be in their career in one, five or ten years? What kinds of allies and partnerships is this person looking for to enhance their visibility and career trajectory?

_____

_____

_____

_____

_____

_____

_____

_____

# » TIP 5

## Learning Prospect & Client Needs
*Filling The Voids*

Would the customers of the 1990s even recognize the customers of today?

As previously mentioned, thanks to the internet, smart phones and social media, today's customers have an ocean of information at their fingertips before any and every decision. They are profoundly aware that they have more choices at their disposal than ever before. As a result, today's customers are more sophisticated, value-conscious and impatient. They are far less likely to be loyal to brands and companies than they once were. Today's customers have real power, and they are not afraid to leverage that power to get exactly what they want. In order to maintain and grow your customer base, it is vital to understand this reality and adapt to new market expectations quickly!

Look around and you will notice that the competition has changed, too. As they keep pace with the more demanding new customer, they too must evolve as the customer evolves. They must continuously refine their offerings as the customer's concept of value changes, which it does, on a dime! Just as important, they must be able to deliver value to this new customer, while producing a consistent profit. Just as you must pay attention to the customer, you must also pay attention to the competition. The one who adapts quickest and most accurately wins!

Starbucks continues its status as one of the world's dominant, successful brands by continuously listening to its customers. They even created a special website for their customers to share ideas. Just as important, they evaluate and implement the best ideas. Direct customer feedback resulted in the company adding pastries to its menu and creating a program that allows customers to place orders before they arrive at the store. These changes appeal to the busy, time-sensitive customers Starbucks targets. In years to come, you can expect other customer-generated ideas to enhance the Starbucks experience.

"You may be disappointed if you fail,
but you are doomed if you don't try."

Aristotle Onassis

## Getting Started

While gut feelings can play a role, it is important to enhance your opportunity for success by continuously reading the needs and expectations of your market. This begins with dialogue with your prospects and customers and can require multiple communication platforms. Ask what they like about your product or service and how you can improve the experience. What would it take for them to refer their family and friends?

Today's companies are using focus groups, online and face-to-face survey mechanisms, smart phone apps and social media messaging campaigns, all with the aim of listening to what has come to be known as the "voice of the customer." Note that this is not merely the responsibility of the marketing or sales team. Front-line employees should be trained to listen to the customer, so that they are better equipped to solve the customer's problems. Everyone in the company must be encouraged to share customer issues and feedback with management.

Selling, marketing, public relations, and customer service, which not long ago were seen as quite separate disciplines, have now merged. As a result, the company must use its customer-facing employees as a conduit to the mind of the customer, in support of these areas. Once identified, respond to these changes throughout the company. Product and service offerings must be inspired in design and function with direct input from the customer. Your front-line employees hold the key to the relationship with your customer!

## The Result of Listening

By design, this new type of constant interaction with a customer must produce two simultaneous results:

First, every product, service and activity within the company must deliver something of value that the customer can easily recognize and experience, on his or her own terms. Your new product and service offerings must be allowed to take shape as business opportunities become apparent. Technology will continue to be a game changer and require you to be agile. Consider how your own expectations and buying process have evolved.

Second, the components of your business offering that no longer deliver value to the customer must be allowed to die. Do not waste your time keeping these products or services alive. However, be conscientious and pay serious attention to how you go about phasing out a product or service in an effort to minimize losses, uncover new trends and create innovative customer solutions.

Continuous reallocation of resources must take place to deliver value that will meet the emerging needs of your customer.

## Focus on the Right Issues

Conducting effective "customer expectation" surveys is critical to your success. Do not presume that you already know which issues are important to the customer. If the survey is focused on areas the customer cares less about, the results can be pointless. Worse, this can lead your team to spend a tremendous amount of time and resources fixing things that do not matter.

A company might review the results and assume that since they did well on nine out of ten issues on the survey, then "all is well." Unfortunately, they would fail to realize that the tenth issue might be the most important to the customer or that the most important issue might not be on the survey at all!

Just as critical, too many "customer expectation" surveys fail to determine whether or not the customer would actually recommend the company to a friend or family member. In an era of purchase decisions that are heavily dominated by online reviews, and particularly those provided by one's own social network, this is a devastating omission.

One of the best ways to have an effective survey is to simply ask your customers to help you create it. This gives them buy-in and increases both trust and honesty. Often, this step in itself leads to sales and referrals!

# The Critical Dimensions

When customers are asked to weigh issues according to their own hierarchy of values, the supplier can gain some insights about where to focus the corporate energies and resources. Feedback from customers must always be gathered in these critical dimensions:

» How important is this issue?

» How are we performing regarding this issue?

Using this approach, the supplier can focus on those core issues where the customer places the most value. The Value-Performance Grid is a simple tool that can be used to graphically portray those results.

# Value-Performance Grid

The Value-Performance Grid allows customers to provide a "weighting" factor for those issues that they value most. The responsive competitor will allocate the bulk of the company resources to improve performance for those highly valued issues regarded as important by the targeted customer, yet where performance is lacking (Quadrant D). They will also minimize resource allocation to those issues that are not as important to the customer, regardless of performance levels (Quadrant A and C).

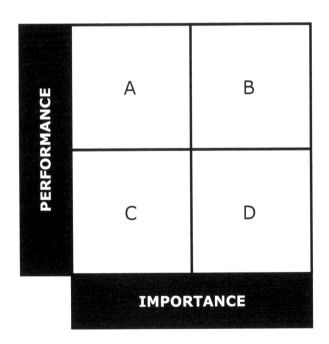

# The Third Dimension

The Value-Performance Grid encompasses a third dimension: the cost associated with delivering value issues. Company resource allocation is dependent on the breadth of resources available to the company, including such items as time and finances. These factors must be weighed in terms of availability, return-on-investment (ROI) and other modeling practices.

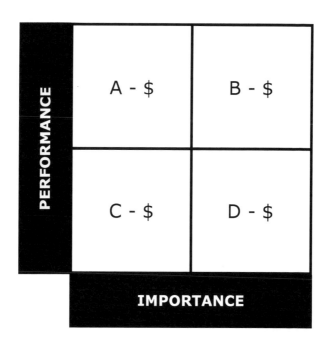

# Example

Blockbuster once dominated the video rental industry, but failed to listen to the market and went out of business. It's quite possible that executives at Blockbuster conducted customer-satisfaction surveys asking whether or not the DVDs consumers rented were scratch-free, or whether the company's staff was pleasant and knowledgeable during in-store conversations. However, if the surveys did not capture feedback from the front lines that customers were becoming more interested in on-line streaming of videos, the surveys would have been essentially meaningless!

Had Blockbuster monitored the market trends and customer feedback, they might have picked up on, and responded to, technological changes that were transforming their industry. By the time they realized what was happening, it was too late to adjust. They went out of business!

# Summary

Companies that are truly customer-focused must maintain a high degree of flexibility and responsiveness as their targeted customers evolve and change. Staying in constant contact with the customer is critical. You should always be attentive to their new needs and expectations and learn to gather the right information to ensure that strategic planning is fruitful.

Keep in mind that many "customer expectation" surveys fail to determine what is important to the customer. The Value-Performance Grid allows customers to provide a "weighting" factor for those issues that they value most.

## Action Item

**»** Involve several important customers and prospects in creating a Value-Performance Grid. Review your results with your team.

_____

_____

_____

_____

_____

_____

_____

_____

_____

# » TIP 6
## Activating Intrapreneurship
*Driving Creative Approaches*

Intrapreneurship simply means nurturing entrepreneurial spirit within your organization. In other words, it is creating a culture of openness and creativity among your team members within specific and agreed upon parameters. The net result is driving profits today!

There is great value to incubate optimization with innovation when building an environment of "open thinking." Those routine, incremental process improvements that result in reducing such items as operating costs or increasing sales represent optimization. On the other hand, innovation results from major, newly discovered approaches to be used either internally or externally.

The issue, however, concerns the gap between what leadership says and what actually takes place. This is not because anyone tries to mislead, however it can be quite trying to shift to a culture where entrepreneurship is activated. Management's fear of people "thinking outside of the box" and their having "freedom" can be daunting. Yet, if done right, this all contributes to team alignment and ultimately satisfying customers' needs.

3M has a long tradition of nurturing both optimization and innovation. Quite simply, 3M is known as a house of intrapreneurship. Management encourages employees to spend upwards of 15% of their work time creating new ideas. Yes, they are allowed to be entrepreneurs within their house of work. One significant success has been that of scientist Art Fry. He strategically repackaged a colleague's accidental creation of a low-stick adhesive and developed it into the now-famous Post-it Notes product in 1980. The result has been hundreds of millions of dollars in profits for 3M.

"It is not the strongest of the species that survive, nor the most intelligent, but the ones most responsive to change."

Charles Darwin

# The Inside Entrepreneur

You don't want a company filled with people who all think, act and decide things in exactly the same way. Not if you want to survive in today's market environment. What you need are people who will assume full ownership and who will restlessly optimize and innovate on behalf of your customers. This should be done within guidelines that are clearly understood and accepted by all involved.

In order to achieve this, they must be given the freedom to fail. We're not talking about failing at anything or the same thing, over and over again. And not about failing in a way that damages your company's reputation or undermines important strategic options. The focus is on the freedom to try new ways of benefiting your customers. When it does not work out, the result is a learning experience, not a slap on the wrist! This is what distinguishes a company that truly nurtures the entrepreneurial spirit from a company that only pays lip service to it.

Even now, it's possible that you may be nodding your head in agreement with these words, without actually accepting that it is okay for your sales, marketing or other departments to fail. The problem arises when we work in generalities, rather than specifics. So let's consider this question: How much freedom do your people have to incubate optimization and innovation? To expand upon that, how is this being measured and what processes are in place for when the result is good or bad?

This can include establishing certain time frames and dollar amounts for creative thinking. For example, each person on your team might be allowed $50 and three hours per week to help improve the company in any way they desire. Whether someone's ideas work or not, you congratulate them for their efforts and ask what they learned. If you do this routinely, your company will flourish!

## Social Media Dilemma

One major area of intrapreneurship many companies still struggle with is social media such as Facebook, Twitter, LinkedIn or other tools. They choose to ban employees from using these during office hours. Why? Management is afraid that someone on the team will make a mistake and put the company at risk. While there is understandable cause for concern, taking these tools away is not the right approach.

Your people should be trained on how to use them safely and effectively. Yes, there will be occasional problems. The question is not whether or not your people will make mistakes. They will. That's the nature of intrapreneurship. The question is how your organization responds to these efforts. That's a balancing act that successful companies will master. And one that sluggish, innovation-resistant companies will ignore.

## Not a Company Size Issue

Intrapreneurship is not just for small, nimble companies. Even industry leaders can and should empower their employees to be "inside entrepreneurs." General Electric is one of the largest companies in the world. It's also widely considered to be one of the best-run. One big reason for that is its ongoing commitment to innovation, a passion with which its former Chairman, Jack Welch, is strongly associated.

Welch rose through the ranks by building General Electric's engineering plastics business as if he was launching his own company from scratch. He and his team made plenty of mistakes along the way, and they learned from those mistakes. That is exactly the spirit that must be supported within your organization. You need an army of "Jack Welch's!"

Here are five important benchmarks that will tell you whether or not your company truly supports intrapreneurship:

**1.** Can anyone come forward with a good idea? If you are not hearing from all the various "front lines" about opportunities for innovation, your company will be at a competitive disadvantage.

**2.** Do you celebrate new ideas, even when they are not implemented? If people feel they will lose standing, or even their jobs, by proposing a new way of doing things, you won't see much innovation.

**3.** How do you handle failure? As long as your employees learn from the failure, and general guidelines were followed, this is an opportunity to pop the cork!

**4.** Do you encourage people to take intelligent risks? A company that celebrates intrapreneurship balances opportunity against the available resources, and balances potential downsides against potential rewards.

**5.** Do you encourage your people to listen to each other, and do you model the behavior of good listening? In today's fast-moving economy, sales, marketing and customer service must constantly communicate with each other, and with top management. If good listening skills are not modeled from the top of the organization down, the organization will be out of sync.

# Example

By celebrating and supporting intrapreneurship, Google has increased the likelihood that their people will spend time doing things that they truly love and care deeply about. For example, Google has implemented a "20% Program," which allows employees to spend 20% of their time at work creating new, innovative ideas. A direct result of this was the creation of Gmail, which now has roughly 500 million users! Today, more than half of Google's product line can be traced to the 20% Program.

# Summary

Intrapreneurship simply means nurturing entrepreneurial spirit within your organization. In other words, it is creating a culture of openness and creativity among your team members within specific and agreed upon parameters. The net result is driving profits today!

How much freedom do your people have to incubate optimization and innovation? Do they truly believe they have the freedom to take intelligent risks while at work? As long as it's calculated, don't punish your team for their mistakes. Instead, discuss what happened, learn from it and motivate them to keep trying! This is what distinguishes a company that truly nurtures the entrepreneurial spirit from a company that only pays lip service to it.

## Action Item

**»** Create specific parameters under which employees have the freedom and resources to develop sales, marketing and/or product ideas that satisfy customer needs.

_____

_____

_____

_____

_____

_____

_____

_____

_____

# » TIP 7
## Knowledge Source
*Beyond Features & Benefits*

Can you remember a time when you were forced to listen to a salesperson regurgitate facts and figures about a product? If you are lucky, they may have even tossed out some product benefits.

Perhaps you noticed the salesperson spoke with all the enthusiasm of a zombie. And at the end of their monologue, you probably just wanted to get away. If you are like most of us, you can relate. In fact, it's probably happened to you more than a few times. You and your team do not want to be mistaken for that salesperson!

Those technical details, the product specs that the salesperson had been forced to memorize, are known as features. The issue with this sales approach is that it keeps the salesperson from asking questions and having a dialogue with the buyer. Today's economy leaves little room for such feature-driven selling, whether it is resulting from the individual salesperson or their company's antiquated training program.

Ace Hardware Corporation is a retailer-owned cooperative with more than 4,700 independent stores throughout the United States. Ace is committed to being the most helpful hardware store on the planet with a focus on do-it-your-selfers. Consequently, the Ace sales associates are hired and trained on the basis of being a true knowledge source for customers, not just providing product features and benefits. This has resulted in J.D. Powers and Associates, the leading research firm in customer satisfaction, ranking Ace Hardware routinely at the top of home improvement retailers.

"When people talk, listen completely.
Most people never listen"

Ernest Hemingway

# Feature and Benefit Dumps

In recent years, effective sales people have learned to avoid the pitfalls of "feature dumps." These are the exchanges that tend to undermine real-world discussions about the possibility of a good fit between buyer and seller. The effective salesperson builds lasting relationships based on offering knowledge-based solutions. Ineffective salespeople, on the other hand, have often hidden behind the (illusory) safety of a barrage of facts and figures.

This problem has been around for a long time. In today's environment, where prospective buyers can instantly Google just about any product spec they might happen to need, your organization has no practical alternative but to move beyond features-based selling. Equally important is for your company not to shift into "benefit dumps." Benefits are important but must be discussed within the context of sharing knowledge with the buyer.

# Become a Knowledge Source

Today, you must identify a range of highly individualized needs and agendas for your targeted buyers. And then create relationships where you offer, not just product and service specifications, but genuine guidance on meeting the deeper aspirations of your prospective customer. Begin by asking open-ended questions. Find out their hot button issues. Dig deeper into their need or desire for this product or service. Do not talk about features and benefits until you have a solid basis of understanding their needs.

Then focus the conversation on educating the prospective customer on what you are seeing in the marketplace. Educate them on how this can (or cannot) benefit them down the road according to the objectives they shared with you. Do not be afraid to direct them to the competition if you don't have the right solution. They will remember you for this and appreciate you sharing your knowledge. Often, this results in positive word-of-mouth and referrals.

## Broaden Your Footprint

If you are used to calling on one particular job title, such as Human Resources simply because you are comfortable talking about their type of issues, guess what? You need to look for new ways to broaden your footprint by calling on other departments. From there, dig deeper to uncover larger, more pressing company needs. When you have identified their needs, look towards your own resources and expertise that you can bring to the table. This should include collaborating with your appropriate team members.

For example, if you learn from the HR manager that the company is looking to lay off employees, because of cash flow issues, you might set a meeting with both your companies' CFOs to discuss the situation. Your CFO might have experience in this specific situation and can share the information. This helps your prospective customer, while elevating your team in their eyes!

If you don't broaden your footprint and help educate, you are a lot like that salesperson that regurgitated product specifications. You are not differentiating your value proposition among numerous targeted departments and you are making it easier for the competition to steal the customer!

# Critical Questions

Be cautious that you and your team don't force the solution. Provide them with knowledge, so they can make up their own mind. Dig deep into what keeps them up at night. The more detailed your answers to the questions below, the easier your transition from feature to knowledge source (teacher) will be:

» What are their hot button issues?

» What are their three most pressing needs?

» How are they resolving these issues?

» What resources and tools do they need?

» What resources and tools can we offer?

» Who else should we target within the company?

This will typically lead you from selling just one product to being their go-to source for all future projects. This is why it is so important for your sales and marketing communications to reach multiple audiences within the company. The more constituencies you talk to, the more gaps you can identify and fill!

# Welcome Complaints

The Technical Assistance Research Project (TARP) discovered that 65% of customers who leave a vendor defect because of service indifference. And 96% of unhappy customers never complain to their present supplier. Therefore, moving from feature to teacher means you must welcome complaints, from both current and prospective customers. Seek problems out, bring all your organization's expertise to bear in resolving them, and you will improve your odds of keeping good customers and gaining new ones. Create a relationship whose foundation is searching out problems and solving them before they become crises.

Avoid the complacency that leads to lost customers. Remember to create relationships with every key constituency within the company you are targeting (or trying to keep as a customer). Find out what they're worried about! Become a partner in addressing those concerns.

# Example

AMS Controls traditionally sold their electronic control systems primarily to the maintenance and production departments within manufacturing plants. The sales team had become overly comfortable calling on these departments using engineering jargon (features and benefits) as a safety net. They were not truly functioning as a knowledge source. Management realized they needed to target C-level decision makers in other departments. Consequently, they broadened their approach making AMS a strategic information source for companies globally.

This has lead to a pipeline of larger deals with longer-term commitments. Most importantly, it means providing knowledge, expertise and resources that address the specific hot button issues of the CEO, CFO, and every other key constituency within their targeted companies.

# Summary

Today's economy leaves little room for feature-driven selling, whether it is resulting from the individual salesperson or their company's antiquated training program. The issue with this sales approach is that it keeps the salesperson from asking questions and having a dialogue with the buyer. The effective salesperson builds lasting relationships based on offering knowledge-based solutions.

Furthermore, if you are used to calling on one particular job title, simply because you are comfortable talking about their type of issues, guess what? You need to look for new ways to broaden your footprint within the organization to earn more share-of-customer.

_____

_____

_____

_____

_____

_____

_____

_____

_____

# » TIP 8
## Competitive Intelligence
*Outwitting The Competition*

You can rest assured that the competition is busy searching for your faults and weaknesses at this very moment domestically as well as globally. Quite simply, they want to sneak between the cracks and steal away your customers. Their ultimate goal is to grow and prosper, and if they damage you or put you out of business in the process, that is too bad.

Further complicating the situation is that corporate restructuring, downsizing and rightsizing have caused a deep fragmentation in our economy. More jobs than ever are being eliminated from companies. The result is an astonishing array of new startup companies estimated to be nearly 1,500 launched each day, along with a massive army of independent freelancers (lone eagles). Both of these oceans swarm with potential competitors who want your customers and are willing to compete on price, service, turnaround time or anything else likely to effect a purchase decision shift.

The bottom line is that competition is striving to be successful and their plan is to steal your customers. You must make an active effort to regularly identify them or at least the key threats. Otherwise, your risk of customer defections will greatly increase. And if they do, shame on you and your team for not being proactive.

Circuit City is a classic example of a company being eaten alive by the competition. The once giant electronics retailer became complacent for over a decade and ignored the competition. They didn't keep pace with competitors in key product segments such as video games and computers. Consequently, they did not properly predict inventory needs (or lack thereof) resulting in low product availability and unhappy customers. Circuit City spiraled from $30 a share down to 10 cents within a two year period, and ultimately filed for bankruptcy!

**"Don't think there are no crocodiles, because the water is calm."**

Malayan proverb

# Let Competition Drive

You can and should use the competition to your advantage. Do not follow them blindly. Your competition can help drive you to new levels of performance and push you to move forward. Understand this and use it to drive your organization's success.

Start by accepting that the competition is visiting with your customers on a regular basis. This is not a sign of disloyalty, but rather of intelligence on the part of your customers. Stay close and learn from your customers what tools they're looking for and you will often learn what tools the competition is providing or trying to provide. Whoever does a better job of reading the needs of customers will have the upper hand in offering the desired solutions.

# Competitive Intelligence

The first step in surpassing the competition is to know them and understand them. This is accomplished by collecting competitive information. Before you collect information, you need to answer three key questions:

» What type of information are you trying to collect?

» How is the information to be obtained?

» How is the information to be used?

Collecting outdated or irrelevant information will not add any value to your bottom line. Make sure you are gathering your intelligence from trustworthy sources and have a strategy for utilizing the information. This will require you to analyze what you found, disseminate what is important and implement a strategy to outperform your competition.

# Collection Timing

Competitive information should be collected on a continuous basis and when needed for specific purposes. An example of collecting continuous information is the grocery store chain that monitors its competitors' daily prices so that it can quickly adjust its own prices accordingly.

The grocery chain may also need competitive information for a specific purpose. For instance, if the chain is contemplating expanding into a new part of town, it will be beneficial to know what the competition is currently doing there. And how might the competition react if the chain encroaches upon their territory.

# What Information

No matter how you decide to collect competitive intelligence, or what your purpose is for it, there are several questions that need to be answered. These include:

» What are the most relevant benchmarks for all competitors in our industry? How are we performing against those benchmarks?

» What is the potential threat of new competitors in the products and markets we are currently serving?

» What competitive threat exists for those products and markets that we would like to serve in the future?

» What are our suppliers' plans? Will they become a competitor in the future? Or will we become their competitor by integrating backwards?

» What are our clients' plans? Will they become a competitor in the future? Or will we become their competitor by integrating forward?

» What potential threat exists from substitute products and services? Are our products and services at risk of being replaced by substitutes?

## Collection Process

Collecting competitive information is best accomplished when a strategy is formulated before the collection process is initiated. The plan need not be complicated, but it should be comprehensive in nature. It should be very clear in terms of its stated purpose and goals. The individuals responsible for the collection process should understand their roles, and the timelines to which they are to adhere.

Competitive information is far simpler to obtain today than even a decade ago due to the availability of online information. It is relatively easy to learn what your competition is telling the world and what the marketplace is saying about your competition. In no time you can gain information by completing searches via platforms like Google and YouTube, and by checking sites that prominently feature customer reviews such as Amazon and Yelp.

Pay particularly close attention to YouTube because this type of visual selling offers a foothold into just about every market these days. If you are facing direct or indirect competition from a young, dynamic new firm, the odds are good that there is some important information about that firm waiting to be found on YouTube.

Once you identify a likely competitor, it is simple common sense to set up a Google Alert that connects you to that company's name and/or its most important products and services. A Google Alert will inform you automatically when the company, product or service is mentioned in online news stories. Here are some of the other information sources of which you should be aware:

» Your own internal data sources. This is often overlooked. It should be your starting point.

» Discussions with employees are frequently an excellent source for relevant competitive information, as well as for designing the competitive analysis. They often have firsthand knowledge of the marketplace, and can provide valuable insights.

» Customers will share marketplace information with you, if you have a strong relationship and they feel that you will use it to better serve their needs.

» Prospects are frequently looking for better options, and if asked properly, they will share the products and services which are available in the marketplace with you, as well as their opinion of the suppliers.

» Lost clients will sometimes divulge why they left you, as well as what they are getting from the competition. This is an extremely important source of marketplace intelligence. Do not overlook it.

» Industry sources such as trade association publications, industry listings and credit services such as Dun and Bradstreet can provide valuable input, as well.

» Government publications are broadly available, including such sources as the US Department of Commerce.

Although there are numerous sources of competitive information, the ones listed above should be considered closely.

# Information Use

The manner in which the collected competitive information is used is perhaps the most critical issue when undertaking competitive intelligence. Warning: Your competition is collecting information on you for similar purposes.

Obviously, the information should be used in an ethical and legal manner. Of equal importance is that the information should be disseminated throughout the organization on a timely basis, so that your team is well prepared to understand and take on the competition. All departments should participate so that they may provide insights on how to benefit from the new information including operations, purchasing, administration, information technology, customer service, marketing and sales.

You should compare your company's strengths and weaknesses with those of the competition. You should discuss what changes need to be made for your firm to continue enjoying its success or what you must do to become successful. Once you find a way to use information about the competition to your advantage, you will have put yourself in a position to outperform them.

# Example

In the very competitive rental car industry companies such as Enterprise Rent-A-Car strive to track benchmarks against competitors including Avis and Budget. They want to know not only what they are doing well, but also, how they are doing it. And then adapt quickly. Typical benchmarks include the following:

» Total fleet size

» Number of vehicles per office

» Revenue per vehicle for each office

» Market-by-market break-even points

» Gross revenue and costs on an area basis

» Rental revenue derived from daily rates and ancillary sales

These records can be found in whole or in part in nearly every major car rental operation.

# Summary

The competition is out there and they want your customers. If you become complacent or overconfident, they will succeed. On the plus side, the competition can help push you to new levels of performance.

Important sources of information about the competition include the internet, your employees, your prospects, your customers and your former customers. If you find a way to use information about the competition to your advantage, you will surely outperform them!

## Action Item

» Identify a threatening competitor and use team members from various departments to collect as much information as possible. Then discuss how this competitor might effect key client relationships and how you can beat them.

_____

_____

_____

_____

_____

_____

_____

# » TIP 9
## CUSTOMERization
*Customer Selection*

CUSTOMERization means identifying and serving what you perceive as your optimal customers.

You should target and prioritize resources to attract and retain your most important prospects and customers. By doing that, you become a more successful supplier and you are more likely to keep your select customer base satisfied. Your customers will come to think of their relationship with you as a positive experience and not just as a series of transactions. They will consider you a value source and referrals will follow.

Some companies execute CUSTOMERization at the sales level. Some do this at the marketing level. Some even synchronize the efforts of the two departments. But very few companies share the goals and best practices of CUSTOMERization up and down the organization. Fully aligning the team around the concept of CUSTOMERization breeds success.

Reed Rubber Corp conducted an analysis of their customer base. They determined that retail walk-in customers constituted a bottom tier category. They ordered little product, and even worse, they interrupted the team who was serving their optimal industrial clients.

The domino effect was massive in that an office person had to check inventory, place the order, carry the order to accounting, forward it to shipping and return it to the front lobby. Four team members were interrupted. The internal processing cost was estimated at $45.00 for the $12.00 sale. Reed decided to "fire" these distracting customers in a simple, non-confrontational manner that protected the company's image. They raised prices for walk-in orders to a minimum of $75.00. In fact, these people were frequently referred to competition with a smile!

"Be civil to all; sociable to many; familiar with few; friend to one; enemy to none."

Benjamin Franklin

# Why CUSTOMERization

CUSTOMERization is crucial to your success. When you pretend all customers are of equal value, you are not able to allocate your limited resources of time and money in a way that best serves your optimal customers. Consequently, you risk losing some of your best customers because your team is pressed too thin and service levels diminish. In fact, the result can be even more devastating as word spreads throughout the marketplace.

The widely acclaimed Technical Assistance Research Project (TARP) study confirmed exactly this point some years ago:

» 65% of customers defect not because of price or product, but rather because of poor service.

» Dissatisfied customers will tell from 9 to 20 persons about the disenchantment.

By implementing CUSTOMERization, you will be better able to serve your ideal clients. As a result of better prioritization of your resources, those ideal clients will be more satisfied, and more likely to continue doing business with you.

A satisfied customer base means the people who buy from you will be receptive to your company gaining a greater share-of-customer. In other words, they will allow you to do more business with them, and be more willing to pay a premium for that opportunity.

You might even find that your satisfied customers will openly spread the word about the pleasure of doing business with your company. And these days, you can multiply out the impact of positive reviews exponentially when you factor in social media platforms.

# Smile to Everyone

Your goal should be to interact with all customers with a smile. However, find a way to eliminate your bottom tier customers without sacrificing any of the goodwill in your relationship. In other words, politely fire them. This takes diplomacy and a clear sense of organizational purpose.

Your employees must understand the concept of CUSTOMERization. They need to accept the value and importance of treating all customers equally, with a 100% service level. We already know that if a customer is not satisfied with the service received, that customer will share the negative experience with many other people. But, don't confuse customer focus with customer abuse. The latter is when customers take advantage of your company. And these are frequently the least desirable customers anyway.

Yet, even though all customers should be treated equally, your team should understand that all customers do not benefit your company equally. In terms of pure return on investment (ROI), some clients will require more time and dollar investment than they will ever give in return. This is when strategically letting go of these customers is imperative to your success.

## Short-Term vs. Long-Term Customers

The first step is to recognize the need to have a targeted portfolio of optimal customers, which includes both short-term and long-term customers. Whether a prospect, or an existing customer, you must learn how to know the difference when targeting them. This is done by asking open-ended questions, such as why they are in the market for your product. If the answer is for an individual project, they are most likely a short-term customer. However, if they are similar to a contractor that may have several more home developments planned in the future, they have the ability to be a valuable long-term customer.

The short-term customer can provide current marketplace feedback, referrals and positive word-of-mouth. The investment required to attract them is limited and the immediate payoff can be great. However, since the value of these customers is not perceived as long-term, minimal effort is made to solicit them as such until their potential changes.

On the other hand, the long-term customer can require sufficient investment in terms of time and money in an effort to attract and maintain them for life, or at least for an extended period of time. Do not let the cost hinder you from targeting these customers. Once you've earned their trust, they will be the ones who help take your business to the next level!

# How to Target

The second step is to develop a framework for analyzing your current customer base. The following factors provide a general guideline.

Review your company mission and goals with the rank-and-file. Be sure there is a consensus. For example, ABC Company's mission is to be the leading supplier of quality coffee products to commercial users in the metropolitan area. The goal is to gain 40% of the market share and maintain 15% pretax profitability.

Analyze the current customer base activity by product or service category. What type and quantities have been purchased over designated time frames? These will vary by company and industry. For instance, ABC Company may decide to focus on various types of coffee purchased over the past 12 months.

Determine the profit contribution per client by product category during the designated time frame. In the case of ABC, over the past 12 months, 25% of the client base purchased 65% of the highest margin coffee category. The middle 50% of the client base purchased 30% of the high margin category, and the bottom 25% purchased 5% of it.

*Note:* This phase of the analysis will only work if you have implemented an accurate pricing and accounting system.

Compare the results of the profit contribution analysis to your stated company mission and goals. Are they consistent? ABC may have 60% market share, but the pretax profitability is only 8%. Is it possible to reach 15% pretax profitability at this market share level? ABC needs to clarify its goals and determine whether or not they're compatible with each other. If not, they need to be modified.

Usually, such an analysis leads to a question like this: Should we (tactfully) fire the bottom 20% of our customers, so we can do a better job of focusing on the others?

## Current Customers

The third step is to develop a promotional strategy that will focus on getting more business from existing customers (share-of-customer), and thoughtfully reduce the number of unwanted customers.

A few tactics for this can include reallocating these customer accounts from your senior employees to newer employees, raising your prices for smaller, less profitable customers or selling these accounts to your competition.

To avoid adverse marketplace reactions, you cannot reduce your service level at any point. You must be more discriminatory in your promotional campaign, so the right types of customers are repetitively attracted.

For example, ABC Company might increase its direct selling effort to those customers who are prospects for purchasing additional high profit products. Furthermore, ABC might discontinue marketing to businesses that have purchased nothing but small quantities of discounted products over the past 12 months.

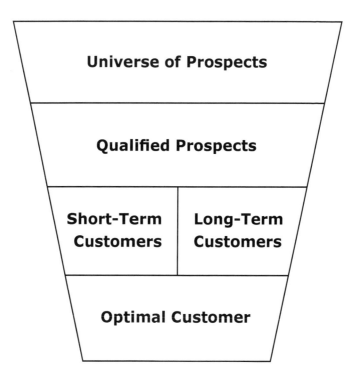

Universe of Prospects

Qualified Prospects

Short-Term
Customers

Long-Term
Customers

Optimal Customer

# Lifetime Customer Value

As mentioned previously, lifetime customer relationships are not forged on single transactions, nor are they exclusively bottom line driven. They tend to be rooted in emotional and personal considerations such as trust, confidence in the values of the service provider and a sense of shared mutual interest. As a result of this relationship, the true customer for life provides both indirect and direct value.

The indirect value promotes:

» Continuity of client presence that represents company stability in the minds of your employees.

» Positive word-of-mouth by the client that will serve a public relations role.

» A sense of family belonging where the client feels a paternal need to help you succeed.

The direct value can be measured in a financial manner:

The neighborhood grocery store provides a good example for determining the lifetime value of a customer. Assume that the average family of two spends $500 a month on groceries. This equates to $6,000 a year, and $120,000 over 20 years.

Remember that in order to sustain a lifetime customer relationship, you must do two things. First, identify and serve what you perceive as your optimal customers. Second, create a positive experience, not merely a transaction.

# Example

The prior grocery store calculation will increase significantly over $120,000 upon further consideration. The first factor is the additional cost to land new customers assuming this customer might leave. Studies indicate that it costs up to five times as much to replace a client as it does to maintain the client. The second factor is the time value of money. Depending on the rate of inflation, $120,000 can actually represent thousands of more dollars.

# Summary

CUSTOMERization means identifying and serving what you perceive as your optimal customers. You should target and prioritize resources to attract and retain your most important prospects and customers. By doing that, you become a more successful supplier and you are more likely to keep your select customer base satisfied.

Remember:

» Treat all customers with a smile.

» Do not confuse customer focus with customer abuse.

» Not all customers benefit your company.

» Identify optimal customers.

» Politely fire unwanted customers.

» Maximize share-of-customer.

» Create an experience, not merely a transaction, for your ideal customers.

## Action Item

**»** Reach out to your targeted customers. Ask them what you could do to make the experience of working with you more satisfying. Listen to what they have to say.

# Action Items

### 1. Company Assessment
*Are We In Alignment*

» Identify a cross section of your management and employee team to participate in a Critical Issues Assessment with a third party facilitator. Upon completion review the results with the team and determine what action plans should be implemented.

### 2. Mission Statements
*The Ultimate Sales Tool*

» Examine the mission statements of your customers and identify the areas of overlap between their mission statement and your own. How can these commonalities be leveraged to win greater share-of-customer within that account?

### 3. The Height of Ingratitude
*The New Customer*

» Have your team identify three clients whose partnership can be further enhanced by technology. Discuss the solutions and the best manner for implementation.

### 4. Targeting Prospects & Clients By Title
*What Are The Hot Buttons*

» Identify a customer where you have only one targeted contact. Then identify at least two new people you could talk to within that organization. Research their backgrounds and then have your team strategically reach out to them!

### 5. Learning Prospect & Client Needs
*Filling The Voids*

» Involve several important customers and prospects in creating a Value-Performance Grid. Review your results with your team.

### 6. Activating Intrapreneurship
*Driving Creative Approaches*

» Create specific parameters under which employees have the freedom and resources to develop sales, marketing and/or product ideas that satisfy customer needs.

## 7. Knowledge Source
*Beyond Features & Benefits*

» Identify three pressing needs within a targeted company based on conversations with their C-level decision makers. Discuss various solutions with your team members and the best approach for implementation.

## 8. Competitive Intelligence
*Outwitting The Competition*

» Identify a threatening competitor and use team members from various departments to collect as much information as possible. Then discuss how this competitor might effect key client relationships and how you can beat them.

## 9. CUSTOMERizaton
*Customer Selection*

» Reach out to your targeted customers. Ask them what you could do to make the experience of working with you more satisfying. Listen to what they have to say.

# About the Author

## Craig Palubiak

Craig Palubiak is the founder of Optim Consulting Group, a management consulting firm that specializes in facilitating business and growth strategies. His clients range from small privately owned to Fortune 500 companies.

Craig has been a business owner (two national firms) and a corporate executive with Enterprise Rent-A-Car where under his guidance commercial leasing became the first national division. He is a noted author, professional speaker and an adjunct professor.

**optimgroupusa.com**

**cpalubiak@optimgroupusa.com**

# About the Author

## Steven Palubiak

Steven Palubiak has been a financial advisor to clients throughout the nation. He is the founder of SGP Capital, a business-advisory firm that partners with financial professionals and their business owner clients.

Steven is a mentor to several start-up companies and actively involved with numerous non-profit organizations. He is an author and professional speaker that has been referenced in Inc. Magazine. He is a graduate of Missouri State University.

**sgpcapital.com**

**steven.palubiak@sgpcapital.com**

# Notes

# Notes

# Notes

# Notes

# Notes